CW01647977

TRIUMPH HOUSE
Poetry with a Purpose

TREASURES FROM WITHIN

Edited by

CHRIS WALTON

First published in Great Britain in 1998 by
TRIUMPH HOUSE
1-2 Wainman Road, Woodston,
Peterborough, PE2 7BU
Telephone (01733) 230749

All Rights Reserved

Copyright Contributors 1998

HB ISBN 1 86161 393 8
SB ISBN 1 86161 398 9

FOREWORD

With the increasing popularity of poetry today it is evident that more and more people are taking up this medium, as a means to express and unchain their thoughts and feelings to others.

Treasures From Within presents to you a gallery of picturesque poetry styles and themes for your enjoyment. It contains a collection of written talent that is both truthful and meaningful to the poet, as each confides in you some of their special and very own treasured thoughts.

With over 100 choice selections of some of the best work being written today, this book is a must for any poetry collection.

Chris Walton
Editor

Contents

VISITING HOURS

. . . The other day
we talked about the important things
in life, like love and laughter,
caring and sharing,
but by your reckoning
the greatest of these is shopping.

The downside is the hereafter
or just simply death
which separates us
from people and things that we love.
There'll be no more hunting for bargains
after the last breath;
no more three for the price of two.
No more Corry Street,
have you thought of that.
(Me, I stifle a cheer)

Oh the uncertainty
of life and the certainty
of death. I am glad you asked me
if I want cremation
with much lacrimation
and my ashes scattered at
Craven Cottage maybe
or kept in a pot by the TV.

Alternatively, a burial with my Brubeck CDs
and several bars of chocolate
for the journey. Yes, I should like that.
No need for crying,
don't be disconsolate.

Please hold my hand I am dying
for a cigarette.

John Gordon

All Too Late

Always to me,
You will be
The loving, caring husband I remember.
So many memories recalled
Cherished within my mind,
Of how perfect our marriage was.
Things went wrong and
I walked away.
Turned my back on the only man
Who'd ever done everything
for me.
Time passed, I thought of you still,
Were you happy with your life?
All I ever wanted,
Your happiness.
Reflecting on knowledge gained
Since our parting,
I know now,
All too late,
What a mistake I made.
I cannot turn back the clock.
I cannot say sorry to you,
Since you have taken your soul
To the angels.

Zoë Fail

STORMY REVIVAL

The rain lashed down on the ocean,
As waves crashed up on the shore,
Gale force winds were howling,
Winter was with us once more.

That haunting cry of the seagulls,
Gliding in land from the sea,
Exhausted from their journey,
They looked as bedraggled as me.

I stared at the gloomy horizon,
Struggling to hold myself still,
Trembling with deep emotions,
My tears they started to spill.

Questions I begged God to answer,
No voice did I hear in return,
I sank to the ground feeling lowly,
When my body it started to burn.

Behold what a wonderful healing,
Revived I praised God, life and home,
Ashamed for being so foolish,
I knew I was not alone.

Christine Shannon

UNTITLED

In my heart,
A lone grey wolf lays before the hearth . . .
Of a castle in ruin.
Dark blood stained stone,
Reflects the moon like splintered bone . . .
The eerie darkness prowling.

Smouldering within embers,
Are the flames the grey wolf remembers . . .
Always warming my heart.
Now sensing your essence,
Blending with my own and ever present . . .
Always together even apart.

Timeless the night,
With its living blackness so bright . . .
Each moment awakening anew.
Feeling the moon stir,
Hunger to scent and taste your fur . . .
Each morning awaking with you.

Nic Dean

THE COUNTRYSIDE

What happened to the countryside,
The countryside I knew as a lad,
When holidays come around,
And we were all so glad.
We'd climb in trees, and ride our bikes
In bare feet we'd catch tiddlers in the dikes,
Next day we'd make a picnic of bread doorsteps and jam
Some lemonade, and some worms in a can.
Then race up the lane, and down to the brook,
Sit fishing with a stick, some string and a
safety-pin for a hook.
I'd lay on the grass, watching clouds in the sky
And wonder where time passed so quickly by.
But now the trees and fields have gone
and I've become a dad.
But I'll always remember the countryside
The countryside I knew as a lad.

Marion M Cook

Horsehead Nebula/Orion Shadow Puppets

Dark, against a sky so bright
Angry like a threat of storm
Birthmark on the night
A memory of when stars are born.

Angry like a threat of storm
What winds howl in that cloud
A memory of when stars are born
With a cry so loud.

What winds howl in that cloud
Do sailors brave the blow
With a cry so loud
Yelling 'Planet Ho'.

Do sailors brave the blow
In ships from distant port
Yelling 'Planet Ho'
Families in their thought.

In ships from distant port
Dying for a want of light
Families in their thought
Dark, against a sky so bright.

Cardinal Cox

A Century Wish

A New Century will soon be with us
what will it bring, I ask
thinking back over the years
that have just flashed past.

Many things have happened
all around the world, my friends
some have made us cry
like deaths of many people and also friends.

We must all now make plans
before the new century starts,
like doing away with land mines
which was dear to Diana's heart.

The fighting, not just in Ireland
must also come to an end,
for life was made for living
not to be destroyed by guns and bombs, my friends.

So to carry on into this new century
we must all have hope and also love
and to teach all our children
to respect what Jesus gave to each of us!

Pauline Haggett

DUNBLANE

Lit candles at every window
The dove is no longer on the wing
Sixteen little ones and their teacher
Now everyone hears the angels sing

One, one mad man that's all it took
On a rainy morning in the gym
Sixteen little ones and their teacher
Thomas Hamilton, all thanks to him

A teacher teaching her small class
Full of happy and smiling faces
Sixteen little ones and their teacher
Still young, still learning to tie laces

Without a warning he appeared
There in the gym, holding his huge gun
Sixteen little ones and their teacher
Then firing started his bullets stung

Frightened children ran everywhere
Many were hurt and many killed
Sixteen little ones and their teacher
Anxious parents came, the lane they filled

A vale of sadness was pulled down
Parents' nightmares because true to life
Sixteen little ones and their teacher
People's hearts were pierced with a knife

Thomas Hamilton shot himself
At least he cannot do it again
Sixteen little ones and their teacher
Now he is hated by all that remain

People laid flowers down the lane
Snowdrops, tulips and many more
Sixteen little ones and their teacher
Remembering them for evermore

The gym was to be demolished
And replaced with a tiny graveyard
Sixteen little ones and their teacher
But people still remain scarred

People will always remember
The scars can never be completely healed
Sixteen little ones and their teacher
In history it now lies sealed

Lit candles at every window
The dove is no longer on the wing
Sixteen little ones and their teacher
Now everyone hears the angels sing.

Fiona Rose

BENEATH THE FLOORBOARDS

Have you ever wondered what's,
Beneath that rotting crumbling wood.
Are they bad or are they good,
Beneath the rotting wood.

Ghosts and goblins, spooks and spirits,
Things from long ago.
Ugly monsters without a head,
Stooping and stumbling low.

Spooks and spirits, phantoms linger,
Underneath the mouldering cinder.
Cockroaches and beetles crawling round,
Moving without a solitary sound.

And when I'm lying in my bed at night,
Hiding under the quilt with fear and fright.
I hear them fighting, screeching, howling,
That ugly sound of them caterwauling.

Laura Evans & Nicola Vowles

Is Death So Bad?

What is death?
My heart is torn
It must be as
Before you're born
Eventually I'll have to go
Is death so bad?
In his eyes no
The world went on
Until then
Nothing did I know
Then I was delivered
In time to see the show
I realised I missed a lot
As older did I grow
It went around
In my head
And had been
If I were dead.

Melvyn Roiter

Bloodsport

I never met her but I sensed her pain.
The media madmen, hungry for gossip,
Tormented her every step of the way.
Like a lonely frightened vixen
She ran away with style
But the hounds closed in for the kill
Her broken body was captured on film
And the Anthem mocks her smile.

Ernie Hoffman

A Certain Love

Without you my life seems dull and empty
My heart is filled with sorrow and with pain
I have to face the truth although it hurts
I'll never see your smiling face again.
You made me laugh but yet you made me cry
You filled my life and soul with so much joy
Now my heart is battered and in pieces
Like an angry child's brand new wooden toy.
We had a special bond, a certain love
No one else could see or understand
How you could give me so much hope and strength
By one touch of your strong, yet gentle, hand.
No longer will I hear that cheery laughter
No more I'll see those sparkling eyes so blue
You're gone but still your spirit lingers on
And still I have the memories of you.
There may be no more talking, no more hugs
You may be gone but I know we're not apart.
I remember everything you've said and done
And you will be forever in my heart.

Margaret Ann Scott

Razor Sharp

Imprisoned by my loneliness
And tortured by my bed
A tape that's never-ending
Plays your voice inside my head
Lost dreams and no tomorrows
Flash your image in my mind
For razor sharp you cut the ties
That did our two hearts bind

Faithful, though the end was bitter
Longing for your touch
Still I grieve and mourn
In silence, loving you too much
Manacled to memories
And plagued by this despair
These tears I cry can't bring you back
For you no longer care.

Kim Montia

TELL ME THE TRUTH?

If you still love me
please let me know
But if you don't
You must let me know
You know I'll let you go, without regret
Just want you to be happy and to be loved

If someone still loves you
Please let me know
If you find someone worth to love
Please let me know
If I'm not the one you thought
Please let me know
Then I'll leave and imprison my soul

If you can't feel my love
Please let me know
If you didn't love me so
Please let me know
But still I have to tell you
You're the girl I really want
You're the only one I've ever loved.

Troy

The Seat

In he shuffles.
Corner seat.
'Six Thirty' - on the dot.
Pint of ale, in grasping hand.
Beer, was once so cheap.

Young men pass.
Pierced and logo clad.
No one dares, encroach the seat.

There he sits, and sips -
Entrenched.
In a once, and better world.

The night creeps on,
and ale induces speech -
Eyes like varnished coals enact,
his polished pit prop tale -
The night he 'Saved William,
and the flood that closed the mine'.

His head now nods,
in fitful jerks.
As sleep impeaches beer.
Men drift off, to diverse mines -
They know the tale so well.

Fag ash falls, on shoddy pants.
Like some precarious pyramid,
from some forgotten Pharaoh's land.
No one sees, nor heeds.

With one last beer.
the bell will sound.
Melancholy clamps,
his dust clad chest.

He wanders off,
as thus he came.
And to the bowl protests -
Reeling back -
And fro again -
back and fro -
again.

'William did you have to die -
and leave me - so alone?'

David R Thompson

Golden Privet In January

What is this brilliant glow?
Why, golden privet,
Glittering in the gloom!
No shaft of sunlight here,
To set the blaze alight.
Houses are hid in mist
And car headlights can
scarcely pierce the haze.
So, do the tiny leaves
Have powers unknown,
To shimmer so
And send me smiling home?

Eleanor Edwards

FREE

Fear looms heavy
Like an image
In the dark
Memories of a past
Trying hard to unfold -
Coming back to haunt
And disturbing
One's peace
Destroying all
In its path!

And there stands Jesus
With arms outstretched
Waiting -
For me!

This foe defeated now -
No more
This body bound
And bent
But free - alive
Like an eagle soaring
Discovering horizons new
Which once
To me
Were out of sight -

A moment to treasure
This -
My new-found
Freedom!

Lynne Livingstone

Just A Memory

Now she's turned
into stone.
Only the stars know
her life story,
Only the stars and moon
look down on her now.
As she sits quietly in the darkness
they alone heard her footsteps
on time's shore.
Now to those who loved her
She's just a memory,
of all those years before.

K Lake

Trying To Avoid Clichés

I stand. Close to the hub of a tractor,
Under an eiderdown of stars.
My hand is beneath the merciless tongue of the cat,
An unusual cat, in the fact that she licks.
The moon is whole, a giant reactor
Of emotions and cycles, to this, our
Great domain. Beyond, the distant river that
Flows and fills our summer place. The water kicks.

Balancing now on the crook of my arm, she is coiled.
The balancing beam tail wrapped about her paws,
My body being warmer than the steel chassis.
While all about, the dogs run, prancing leaves.
The night is deathly quiet, the cliché spoiling
The description. Like Dali's painted drawers
I see myself. Odd to look at, look if you want, not too classy.
Living in another drawer now, the one nearest the heart of the me's.

Vicky Ind

Love

How can love be described,
It's how you feel deep inside,
Nothing is too much trouble,
Knowing someone has burst your bubble,

Loving and caring day by day,
Watching children while they play,
Being able to give someone a kiss,
Can make your heart jump and miss.

The smile on a loved one's face,
A ballet dancer's care and grace,
Love is a chain reaction,
Shown in every little action.

Love has been handed down,
To each generation,
Through many many years,
Of happiness, joy and tears.

P White

Tomorrow Comes Too Soon

The sun, the moon, the stars
the sea,
These elements used to remind you
of me
As summer fades into a cold
grey morning
Tears of heartache slowly falling
echoes in my mind, my name you are
calling,
Your voice so calm it cannot be,
was I so blind I could not see
my thoughts cast back to a sunny day
clear skies bright colours, mountains
of green
cascading water falls into a stream
and me next to you, it was like a dream
As we sit on the beach and stare
out to sea,
you remind me our love will never be,
but the sun, the moon the
stars and the sea
These elements will always remind
you of me.
Alone with my thoughts, I stare at
the full moon, for all my tomorrows
will come too soon.

Barrie Loughran

Rite Of Passage

I have walked this path many times.
I have walked it when the snow has
cloaked the winter light to make the daytime dark
and when the colours of the growing wheat turn
beneath the scattered notes of the rising lark.
I have heard echoes hanging on the years.
The voices of children woven
on the black cloak fabric of the laden air
and the howl and cry of late autumn's laugh, lay
the years cracked and fading soul to bare.
I have danced to the moon's timeless waltz.
The wax and wane of estuarine
tides, bedecked with goldeneye and smew
and the lunar halo surrounds the blunted
silhouette of the owl eclipsing the shrew.
I have touched the passing seasons.
Spring rain and sun baked earth, the soundless
fall of wet leaves and the iced grip of winter rime,
a rite of passage, perpetual, beyond
when I have walked this path a final time.

Ian Gent

A Poem For John

Quite a few months ago, I met an English gentleman,
I always knew he was special, but I didn't realise then
How generous and helpful his nature really is,
To get to know him better - well, it's simply a bliss,
He likes to help all the people, he's caring, gentle and kind,
It's rather difficult somebody else like him to find,
He certainly enriched my life in these recent months,
He also helped me in so many ways - and that's what really counts,
We formed a special friendship which I value so much,
And what's more - it has purely sisterly - brotherly touch,
He's introduced me to hobbies I've never done before,
And once I've got the hang of them I want to practice them even more,
they are golf, bridge, and dancing and I love them all,
Also I want to be good at them - that's my recent goal,
John, I wanted to thank you for everything you've done for me
Regardless the circumstances I'm here to help and support you -
you'll see,
Meanwhile I pray for your pleasurable, satisfying and blessed
with contentment time always to be.

Anna Bayless

Patience

Patience has an upturned face,
Of radiance and trust.
That's born of love and wisdom.
Of all things kind and just.

Patience is a knowing,
Deep within the waiting heart
That order draws a perfect course
Upon the spirit's chart.

Patience love the present hour
Whatever it may hold.
Savouring its offering
Of spendthrift or gold.

Patience is expectancy that
Good is ever true.
That love's abundance flows
Unchecked, and constantly to you!

William Price

Climatic Change

What once was dry land
Will become wet lands
What once was warm climates
Will become cold
Deserts and tundras
Will flood without warning
Forests and woodlands
Shall all disappear
Mountainous ridges beneath, the seas
Will rise up again
To be touched by the splendour
Of our nuclear sun,
Of all that was known
Shall all disappear
Cultures and nations, lost in the sands
Political viewpoints being old news
Religions corrupted being destroyed
Waters all out being deployed
Drowning our sorrows
And trapping our souls.

Gary Ritchie

THE QUARRELLING FAIRIES

On giant toadstools in a wild fairy ring.
Sat four forest fairies, arguing,
Debating the fate of their home, the woodland,
Poised with her magic, in her tiny hand,

The fairy of Summer broke forth her spell,
To make the land hers, and the sunshine's as well.
Flowers bloomed forth from rich and dark soil,
Elves carved rose petals in ceaseless toil.

The fairy of Autumn was not having that,
Hit her over the head, whilst she was out flat,
Took over the land with her own ideas,
To fulfil everything that she'd wanted for years.

She asked Weather Wizard for climate of cold,
Spray painted the tree leaves in orange and gold,
Outraged at this nonsense, young Spring stepped in,
Having spiked Autumn's tea with a great deal of gin.

As Autumn retired off, poorly to bed,
Seizing the chance to now get ahead,
Commanded the blossom to sprout pink and white,
Whipped up the wind enough for a kite.

'Enough!' Winter said, took Spring in a strangle,
Squeezed out her body through an old mangle.
Left at long last, to her own device,
Silver sprinkled the land in snowflakes and ice.

From a blood ruby poppy, amazed at this scene,
Peeped her sparkling majesty - the fairy queen
Taking overall command of the job now in hand,
Silenced them all and took over the land.

Apportioning control to each for a season,
Decided this just, and did not question reason.

Sometimes if you're lucky, the fairies are seen,
Changing the land from platinum to green.

Andrea Whytock

LIFE IS A WAR

Her thoughts like a snake slithered through
the dark corridors of her mind.
The neon sign across the street,
bathed her room in an orange glow.
Her heart was broken in pieces.
Funny jokes and laughter,
couldn't make her laugh,
They crackle like flames in the fire.
Her life was going down the drain,
like rainwater in the gutter.
She had no control over her life,
It went in twists and turns,
Until she found herself dumped
with a suitcase on a railway station.
A shabby room in a shabby hotel summed up her life;
No one gets off scot free;
Everyone seems to suffer
some sort of heartbreak or another;
You can build up as many defences as you like
against this life, but life is a war,
tearing them all down.
Life checks out at the grave.

Kevin J Herbert

LONELY

I sat in a room all alone
Watching the curtains fly, to and fro
All day in this dreary house
Not even a sound from a single mouse
How good I would feel if I had faith
And had some loving warm embrace
How sweet I would feel if I could love.
Have someone to talk to except God above.
With that I placed my face in my
hands and wept.
I cried that much until I slept
And then I woke to a sudden moan.
But yet again I was on my own.

Carmen Weston

Kim

November eve wind so cold
  Kim came to say hello
Hair in dance eyes aware
  Smile freely shared.
Taking winter walk
  Time slips by with valid talk
Healing tree Kim did touch
  Warmth felt so much
To shed spiritual light
  Throughout the night.

Alan Jones

God's Secret

It's autumn time.
The leaves all glow.
Before the winter
when we have snow.
God comes out
With dustpan and broom.
he sweeps the leaves,
to be gone soon.
Up and down
they dance and fly.
Down to the earth
and up to the sky.
The trees, splendid time
of year,
We soulful people
shed a tear.
To see the end become
the start,
new beginnings . . . thou art.
Onto the winter,
Buckets of snow
and ice and hail.
God dost throw.
Behold God cleans
our roads and streets.
Our home is cleansed,
our heart beats.
Happy as ever, to see
the sun.
Each new spring flower,
Our first one.
The promise is kept,
Pleasure and sun,
In our cleansed world
May we have fun.

Gillian Wade

Mad March Days In Crawley Town

Pausing to rest a while on sun-warmed seat,
Basking in sunshine that took by surprise
Crowds of spring shoppers swelt'ring in the heat,
Hoping to find something just the right size.
Through Memorial Gardens to County Mall,
Mem'ries of wild March wind whipping its way
Breeze past the mind's eye with instant recall
How fearful elements one awesome day
Along the Boulevard, blew dust and dirt
Swirling, whirling round the feet of the throng
Clinging to hedges and walls as they skirt
Their way to C & A's while bowled along.
Students and secretaries fleeing parks
For havens of office, college or 'Marks'.

Barbara Winstanley

THE NEAP TIDE

It cools the oppressive summer heat,
like the bathing of a feverish child.
Cautiously progressing, perplexed,
hesitant, not reckless or wild.

Stealthily searching,
filling and flooding, incessant.
Amiable in nature,
not forceful, but persistent.

the Neap tide laps against boats,
cradles, comforts and reassures.
Caressing the lower levels of the coast,
gently embracing the beach once more.

The sun baked estuary mud,
finally is saved from its grief.
Irrigated by the cooling water,
it whispers thankful relief.

At the modest height of the tide,
the water falters and falls.
Departing as lethargically as it came,
to the sound of the marsh birds' scavenging calls.

The neap tide, true to its nature,
always arrives late in the day.
Always late for the party,
always too late to play.

Barely in time to hear the rapt echoes,
of the people just departed.
With a vision of what might have been,
the neap tide ebbs away, broken hearted.

Keith Arnold

One For The Road

The clocks tick with the silent hours
As have the years past with the distant laughter
A friend drifts like the tumbling seasons
But the ones that mean my life stay.
As the ice melts with God's inspiring rays.
The minds are weak.
But the heart still smiles
We have raised our glasses for some victorious trials
Drank to our health, shared our tears
Loved the women who have disappeared over the years
Friends, our life has been varied and rich.
As we have had some monumental trips.
Now's the time to hug once more
And let god take us to Heaven's back door.

Richard Scott

More Than Just A Channel Port

To those of you who're passing through
I'd say take time to see the view
From Dover's famous white chalk cliffs
Witness to history's passing tiffs

From Roman times this island race
Repelled invaders face to face
The narrow strip of open sea
Invites both friend and enemy

Saxons and Normans left their mark
A towering castle, tall and stark
Against the skyline, strong and bold
Broke hearts and made men's blood run cold

There's more to see than steamer funnels
Beneath the ground defensive tunnels
Recall the most ingenious way
Napoleon's troops were kept at bay

And when on Dunkirk's crowded beach
The British troops stood out of reach
From Dover, Ramsey's makeshift fleet
Secured a victory from defeat

A Heritage Centre marks the spot
Where Romans used to scheme and plot
Now if the past's hard to relate
You'll find it here brought up to date

So don't be hasty when you book
Take time to stop and have a look
Don't let this be your last resort
It's more than just a Channel port.

Stuart Gooda

So Precious

I feel that the battle
Was lost so long ago
I feel that we were warned
But didn't want to know

Why couldn't mankind
Take heed of the warnings
Its too late to change
When the last day is dawning

So take to your heart
All the words
That I write
Mother nature's so precious
We must treat her right.

Alan Green

A Willow Tree

My willow tree sheds its green reluctantly
Each silent, drifting leaf
Falls like a tear
Shed for the lost splendour of the year.

Don't weep, old tree
With bare boughs stark against the winter sky
You will not die.
Keep watch over the sleeping earth
'Til spring brings re-birth
And you are clad again in greenery.

Joan Ierston

TIME

Beloved, now are we the sons of God.
Ye observe days, months, times and years!
For we are but of yesterday and know nothing
because our days upon earth are a shadow.
the angel said there should be time no longer.
For a thousand years in thy sight are but
as yesterday when it is past, as a watch in the night.
the Lord shall reign forever.
that which has been is now,
that which is to be hath already been.
Jesus Christ the same yesterday, today and forever
There is a natural body and there is a spiritual body

Jesus the Son is the natural body.
Christ the *Son* is the spiritual body.
Jesus was on earth 33 years
Christ is from everlasting to everlasting.

The Ven Bede (673-735) should have
used Jesus' name for measuring time -
'Before Jesus - After Jesus'.
There was no period 'Before *Christ'* as
the Christ is the S*on* in the Holy Trinity
with God and the Holy Spirit from the beginning.
Jesus, the son of Joseph and Mary discovered
Trinity when he lived on our planet - and proved it!
'For God speaketh once, yea twice
yet man perceiveth it not.' *Christ* and *Jesus?*
'Ye shall know the *truth* and
the *truth* shall make you free.'

No millennium, age or time will have
any new ideas to teach mankind of
the light of *truth* - which has always been within reach.

Dilys Baylis

Descent

As I made my way down
From the sundrenched summit,
I felt my limbs drag and my heart grow heavy;
From the enjoyable plateau of past and future,
I made myself present for roll-call next day.
And nor was it merely regret at descent,
But an absence of feeling
Whose unknown presence had lifted before,
Filling myself with a welcome energy
That strengthened my back and curved my insides.
Grumbling I descended to shaded colour
As the budding mountain came greying stone,
Soaking up the social stress once more;
And I felt my life begin to beat much faster
As I settled back in my particular groove.
Yet later whilst I viewed that mountain,
The colour returned with different sight,
Restoring the energy to my wanting mind,
Filing the memory as a sacred charm,
As a light in the lee of the mountain.

Andrew Smith

Day And Night

Oh the
summer
skylark
you
once
were.

Swallows
and
swifts.

And nightjar

Oh the summer
with
you
on my mind

Safe in the
knowledge

That -
I've known
better times.

Philip Allen

Forever Friends

I passed you in the street today
We stopped and talked a while,
Of inconsequentialities
It was good to see your smile.
Seems like ages since I saw you
Yet nothing's really changed,
Another joy, another heartache,
Another wrinkle gained.

In the spring we laughed at life
Went walking in the rain,
Made plans and didn't stick to them
Chose wrong and paid in pain.
In summer when the sun was bright
We sunbathed on the beach,
And watched our children growing up
Our goals all seemed in reach.

When autumn came with golden leaves
The nights grew dark and cold,
Snuggled safely in our homes
Not now quite so bold.
Now winter's here we're not so young
How quick the years have sped,
I remember all our yesterdays
Like snapshots in my head.

Our friendship's deep and special
As it's stood the test of time,
We've shared so many memories
You're the rhythm to my rhyme.
All through the seasons of our lives
We've weathered storms together,
So when the children lose in love
I say 'Friendships last forever.'

Sally Malone

SHARING

Come and sit and talk with me
in that old familiar way,
Let's sit down and have some tea,
And you talk about your day.

Did you meet anybody special?
Someone to make you smile?
Did you make somebody happy?
Just for a little while?

Are you tired? Are you lonely?
How is the world with you?
Come and sit beside me,
And we can talk it through.

Maureen Cunningham

A Dream Of Mammy

The harvest moon is risen above the Campsie hills,
a landscape bathed in moonlight, belies the evening chills.
The trees they shimmer and reflect, the softly falling rain,
I see the place where mammy rests, and still I feel the pain.

The grass is growing once again, on the grave of Mammy Coyle,
she lies for all eternity in Cawder's rich dark soil.
the little rabbits frolic, and nibble Mammy's flowers,
I see the mirth in Mammy's eyes as they feast away the hours.

I see the stone, dark sentinel, and smooth the marble grain.
I trace the legend carved in gold, despair pervades my brain.
Her name is carried on the wind and whispered by the breeze,
To echo still the sad refrain of weeping willow trees.

I scan the heavens myriad stars to look for Mammy's light,
A figure gazing upwards communes the long dark night.
My silent vigil ending, I find no truth above,
for Mammy's light is deep within, her legacy is love.

This joyful revelation, this vision makes me whole,
she lights darkest corners, the recesses of my soul.
For Mammy lives in mind and heart, in everyone she knew,
her light is life's own meaning, her love comes shining through.

I turn towards the brooding hills, the sky is tinged with gold,
God's new day is promised, its beauty I behold.
My eyes survey the view she loved, as dawn begins to break,
I see her face in every flower, and I become awake.

David Jones

Come And Adore Him

I love you, Lord Jesus so meek and so mild,
This I sang every Christmas when I was a child.
I believed every word, I knew it was true
that he came down to earth to save me and save you.

I liked the stories of shepherds and wise men
And I wish I could have been with them then.
The manger He was put into with warm new-cut hay,
The star overhead to show people the way.

They all came to worship and to adore,
And prayers and praises will rise evermore.
And so in my life He is always my guide,
He has to come first, and in Him I abide.

Flora Lake

ALIENS VISIT THE NEWSAGENTS

The local newsagent he did say,
He had two strange customers the other day,
They had come from outer space,
To pay a visit to observe the human race,
And some newspapers they wished to buy,
The inquisitive newsagent politely asked why,
They replied by scanning the newspapers they could see,
Of what sort of life it would be,
If they ever decided to stay here for good,
However they doubt that they ever would,
They have not been on earth for very long,
And have already noticed something is wrong,
They say that humans look at them in a strange way,
As if they do not want the aliens to stay,
Humans are not used to seeing aliens here,
And probably think they have something to fear,
The aliens insist they have only come to learn,
And promised there is no need for any concern,
With that they bid the newsagent farewell
Giving him a story to his customers he could tell.

Martin Westcott

Road Raaage

'Hey I'm here!'
'Behind this wheel!'
'Hey I'm here!'
'Pushing steel!'

'I'm on a fix for more speed,'
'So don't go so slow!'
'I hate Sunday drivers'
'And letting you know.'

'Hey I'm here!'
'Behind this wheel!'
'Hey I'm here!'
'Pushing steel!'

'The engine is revving,'
'I'm crunching gear after gear,'
'The speedo is racing,'
'I'm right up your rear.'

Marcus Tyler

My Pet Hate

All creatures dwelling on the earth
Have their rights and have their worth,
Flyers, runners, swimmers, gliders,
But what I really hate, are *spiders.*
Spiders, spiders everywhere
Across my face and in my hair,
Weaving their autumn inter-net;
They have invaded, and I've met
Whole families swinging through the air,
Hurrying, scurrying here and there,
Bridging chasms past believing
Nor plant, nor bush, nor post they're leaving.
In gossamer webs fat 'grand-dads' lie
For the unsuspecting autumn fly.
And misty morning grass is spattered
With webs as though small feet have pattered.
And soon this world-wide web of spiders
Runners, climbers, swingers, gliders,
Has autumn all tied up and bowed
Within their all-encasing shroud.
And indoors too they've come apace
Their winter quarters to embrace,
And the *darling child* a-visiting me
When I asked his mum to tea,
Was sure to find what I had missed
As in his childish voice he lisped,
'Guess what I spy, Auntie dear,
A cobweb on your chandelier!'

Norah M Field

THE BEAST UNTAMED

The evil released,
The goodness forgot.
The man knows no cure
For the ailment he's got.

He goes through such pain,
Pain from inside,
Feelings and life
Are all pushed aside.

The hurting doesn't stop,
It tears through his heart.
His body together,
His emotions apart.

He yearns for such freedom,
To fly with the dove.
The Beast untamed,
The man in love.

Alex Hulme

Giving Up

'Get on with your life' she said,
but what the hell does that mean?
What can I get on with? . . .
or, more grammatically,
with what can I get on?

Shall I clean the windows -
study theology -hope for a partner -
paint my toe-nails -
become a Buddhist -
or go on writing
things that no one wants to read?

'Get on with your life!' -
as though it were a piece of knitting
lying somewhere, unfinished . ..
as thought I could retrieve it,
strictly following instructions,
until there was a garment,
unlovely - out of date,
one would not want to wear.
I must have been
already sick and tired,
to have put it down.

She could have said
'Don't get on with your life' -
'It's not a waste of time
to watch the sky for hours,
or wonder in a child-like way,
about the unknowable'

I was born for that,
but slept uneasily,
for seventy years!

Marie Courtez

RAIN

The Nation was mourning
That Sunday morning
Skies were black
And lightning crack'd
The thunder rolled
As news unfolded
Torrential rain
Seared the lane
Mingling with tears
For all her lost years.

Margaret Dunning

HRH Princess Of Love

We light a candle
In our hearts,
And recall memories
Of our beloved one.

We think of William
And Harry too,
But even though she's gone
She's with them in their dreams.

How can one person
Have so much love?
And help so many people
In such a short life?

So we say our farewell
And hope you rest in peace
You were an irreplaceable beauty
And in our hearts you'll remain.

Caroline Williams (13)

COUPLE

I met them on the road,
every day, wet or fine,
tottering along, foot by foot
together, always together.
He led the way.
She followed, a few paces
behind.
He sometimes complained;
muttering in his beard
and waving his stick.
She never complained
but gave sharp glances
of muted wrath.
And still they blundered on,
going nowhere,
from here to there -
a well-trod path.
Missing him for some time,
I thought him dead
and wondered how she coped
alone.
But, not his turn to die,
he still wandered,
old and lonely.
It was the dog
had slipped his leash
and left his bone
to dry.

Leo Lee

Sweet Intoxication

There's an effervescent feeling in the air today;
An ever widening circle, it sweeps all else away,
Engulfing all it touches, like a boiling bubbling river,
Exciting all the children; making old hearts quiver
With fervent expectation.
A big tent is now erected upon the village green,
And tonight - so posters tell us - Earth's finest show is seen.
There's caravans and cages, all dotted round the lea
And trampolines and tightropes being tested expertly
With intensive dedication.
At last it is the evening; the crowds are pouring in,
The last seat's being taken as the procession's entering.
Fanfares, silver sequins, and diverse costumes bright,
Lead their dancing horses; - gives spectacular delight
To gasps of adoration
Dwarfs and clowns fool around, with elephant acrobats;
The liberty horse, with feet held high; mimics the tightrope
On backs of Palominos, the cowboys stage a show
And flying trapeze artists are watched from far below,
In fear and trepidation.
Now the ring is darkened; soft music floats from afar.
The Spanish Lipitzano, embracing every sound,
Displays a graceful Piaffe; then his 'Airs above the ground'
With powerful inspiration.
Thus, with fetlocks and with feathers, this magical display
Bids its last farewells in glittering array.
The marquee now is empty, and they start to pull it down,
But always we'll remember when the circus came to town
With sweet intoxication.

Patrick E Woodley

HANDS

Hands that rocked my cradle as a helpless mite I lay,
Hands that washed and fed me through each unconscious day.
Hands that gave a meaning to the face that shone above,
these so linked together a babe's first sight of love.

Hands that worked and fed me throughout my schoolboy days,
They blessed or they admonished to prove the better ways.
With a brave attempt at calmness they packed my soldier case,
But they trembled, and they fluttered beneath the tear-stained face.

I held those hands so tightly an attempt to calm their fears,
But knew that once I'd left her there'd be another rush of tears.
Hands that loved - hands that cared could do no more for me.
Fate and Adolph Hitler had usurped their authority.

They tried to hold me back God knows how hard they tried.
But now the tears were restrained, 'twas the Mother soul that cried.
Through four long years of misery I missed their loving care,
But knew throughout my exile those hands were joined in prayer.

They signed the Cross of Jesus on worried brow and frame,
Invoked His Blessed Mother and whispered oft my name
She dreamed the dream of nightmares which proved that I were dead,
She awakened in her darkened room and prayers again she said.

I wish that I could now give back some part of which was given,
'Twas not material gifts she gave nor for those would I have striven.
It was some blessed part of her through spiritual channel to be,
That I count most of all my worth which she bequeathed to me.

When the 'Last Rites' have been offered and this once ruddy face
grows pale,
May those blessed, precious work-worn hands lift me through the Veil.

Harold Gill

The Old House

This old house will shelter you
From raging winds and winter storms
Come live in this house where love has been,

Strange enchantment through these windows
A path to a door in the twilight
Calling you, come live in this house
Fill these rooms with light
for your delight,

Moonshine on oaken stairs I see
sunbeams through these mullioned windows be,
Come live in this house, where love has been.

Phyllis Barton

Glass Jar

You filter through the room
Like the presence of an omen
A serpent in the form of a man

The seed of my hatred
Is buried in a glass jar
And shatters before reaching you
Falling like the autumn leaves
To be crushed beneath your feet

You stand undefeated
Walking upon the water
Which I can only drown in.

Polly S Naher

Bands Of Gold

They wear a band of gold
But they never make you happy
And you'll only see them smile
When they inflict their wrath
Slapping tickets, madly, onto glass
Always so solemn, never breaking the mould
Always willing to write their name and number
But it's an expensive autograph.

You can't park there, it's a ticket zone
But everywhere is, when gold band's on the road
Surely they have compassion
But it's a sacred side to show
What does it matter, we'd only offer excuses
And onto deaf ears they'd fall
But gold bands have a job to do
We could really do without them though
The ubiquitous traffic warden.

John McIlhoney

UNANSWERED

I spend the time - though not in rhyme -
To write someone a letter.
A friendly one, all said and done
I couldn't word it better.

Wait for reply, but time goes by
Not even a quick phone call.
Some word or two to answer you
A notelet with a scrawl.

Though I'm not there, around the square
Waving protest banners.
Yet more and more I do deplore
The lack of decent manners.

Molly Rodgers

Muddled Up World

Muddled, confusion
what is it about
Time, love, hate, affection . . .
what's one to do
in this muddled up world.
A world of hate
a terrible place
for what in the future
is there to face.
Is there love,
happiness and joy
or is there hate, disgust
and people that annoy.
The moving of time
the knowing of death
but what lies in the future
what lies in the past
as time slips away
we have to move fast.
Is there a quickness,
a timing or a test
to which we are holding
to which we detest.
If there is such evil,
such anger, such pain
then what is the point
of living in vain
or such of a point
of going insane.

Fiona Senior

INFRA HATE/RED

White-knuckles clench in reflex
'red-mists' begin to rise
it's hard to focus - logically
as 'hatred's' fire flies
So burn the eyes with crimson
twitching-sockets boiling blood
till scarlet is the state of mind
when 'hatreds-juices- flood . . .
Torments in the psyche
set emotions creatures 'riled'
free the dogs of *hate* 'pell-mell'
untamed and running wild!

Barry Howard

FINIS

Days of meditation
Wear hard on my soul,
After weeks of isolation
Your heart is cold.

Feelings of disgust
I withdraw from your touch,
Words of mistrust
Said lightly - mean much.

Days of happiness
Now torture my mind,
Go back to your other
Leave nothing behind.

Sophie S Bennett

Her Home

The raining blows about my head
Like warm red rain
Flooded with love
Down my face and brain

As you suffocate my life into nothing
With such innocent skill
And ridicule my being
Which makes me fainting still

As you lecture me of what I am
And cut me to bleeding peel
Your fever runs cold sweat
Over the hurt that I feel

Then like a changing breeze
I kneel to say I love you
And will do whatever you please
Just to hear it from you too

As we hold on to each other
Blinding each with our salty tears
I hope that this will not be the future
Of a life with too few full years

The room shuts its door for the present
It's the past it should open for
Yet it doesn't matter for the peasant
The person you've butchered galore.

Frank Samet

A Christmas Nightmare

Christmas is near what do I do
I have no money to buy gifts for you
We get together as a family
And make decorations for our tree
The kids sit up the table and make
A colourfully iced Christmas cake
They get excited this time of year
They don't realise everything's so dear
The adverts on TV show lots of toys
Dolls and cars for girls and boys
They point and say 'Mummy I want that
Under the tree in my Christmas sack'
But what do I tell a child so small
That he may not get any gifts at all
'Wait and see' I always say
Christmas is still a few weeks away
To children this time goes by slow
And fast for you, this you know
On the fireplace the stockings hang
For you to fill with us much a you can
But sorry I am afraid to say
There will be tears on Christmas day
when all the things on your list
are just a blur because we're all *drunk.*

Tina Nunn

The Nightmare

Within the gloomy night of her mood,
Her soul's spirit fell from the edge of the world.
        On melancholy's lesser planet,
        The bright world of ironic sunshine
In heedless mirth abandoned her.

The crimson earth, the fire of her wrath,
Scorched deeply within on her frail naked feet.
        The plaintive voice, her soul, the tortured,
        In howling winds, the gale of passion,
The earnest cries for peace subdued.

In doubt she turned her dark frenzied head
Unto either side, then behind and before . . .
        In anguish tossed her raven tresses,
        Through the dusk of indecision,
Her confidence lost, sped blinded on.

Uncalmed, untamed, her panic up reared;
A threatening mask of hideous fear
        Loomed, kindled eyes white hot and burning,
        From which leapt deeds as callous phantoms,
Like shapeless apes with lengthened claws.

Within her weary deep inward eye,
The Devil's long hands in vision stretched forth,
        Yet greener than the hide of reptile,
        Clasped the sword of hell's destruction
With fingers giving birth to flame.

Within the Devil's eyes was the night,
With vision transformed in agony's gaze.
        The sands below on shore lay brazen,
        Smouldering deep as sunset's embers,
And twined with Vipers' worldly spite.

The livid sea uneasily wreathed,
Luring her soul in despair in its tide.
        To bosom black as mortal sinner,
        Tossing foam tormented tears
In whirlpools of eternity.

Above bemoaned the storm smitten sky,
Low clouded brows in judgement's frown,
        Devouring sins in fangs of starlight.
        Though worldly courage conscience gnawed
For Heaven's realm the corridor.

Dorothy Mary Allchin

My Ex-Girlfriends

Each night, as I lay alone in my bed
The only memories that I can find
Are those of the ex-girlfriends that I dread
As like a swarm of wasps they are unkind.
They have peeled back the soft shell of my mind
And read ev'ry one of my secret fears
Then aimed the savage stings in their behinds
In order to extract my bitter tears,
The buzzing of their complaints hurts my ears,
I'm 'too thin', 'too apathetic', 'too poor'.
And this is all my fragile ego hears,
They jeer at how little I can endure,
Therefore I have a nest of memories
Good for nothing except to taunt and tease.

Chris Scriven

THE SUMMONER

I thought death had brushed past my feet
But it was you dressed in a black cloak
Running away with my heart.
The fragrance of your love
Is like the scent of death
The rhythm of your heart beats like the drums
Summoning my execution
You kill this spirit and leave the empty vessel
To wonder alone.

Babley K Nissa

Room 101

There is a room 101 inside every one of us
denouncing
all those we love
everything that we stand for
yet we are afraid to enter that room
lest we find nothing
The nothingness of ourselves - our lives
Pictures on the walls
of things we would rather forget
Hung high out of our reach

And a voice we cannot silence
Repetitive and all accusing

I cannot escape
Only when released - if released
will I be free.

Clive Cornwall

THE DOORS

One door shuts another opens
That's what the people say
A very clever proverb
For it often works that way.

A sudden change of fortune
A sudden slender purse
And we all think fate is cruel
And that it couldn't be much worse.

And when we feel our patience
Is very sorely tried
Quite suddenly a door appears
That's opened very wide.

When doors are shut before us
We're bound to feel depressed
Quite suddenly another opens
We find it's for the best.

D Sheasby

Pet-Hate Syndrome

Is our tolerance level falling?
Or is it that the pace of life has escalated to such an extent,
We are all rushing around like lemmings, trying to avoid that
Proverbial cliff.
Circumstances however, afford this lack of patience;
The *Pet-hate* syndrome.
I see red, when driving within the speed limit,
Having the right of way, trying to be observant,
When suddenly a surly Volvo-driver, pulls out of a side road in front
of me;
No regard for the highway code, or fellow driver,
As my anger increases, I find myself tailgating for a while.
After filling my trolley in the local supermarket,
I glance for the smallest queue, on reaching the appropriate check-out,
Not only do I find a *First Day* trainee, OK everyone has to learn,
But the till roll has run out and the code-gun is inoperative.
Whilst holding on the phone, for one of the *Boards,* Electric or Gas,
Why do we have to listen to Vivaldi's Four Seasons being crucified,
Then an interruption tells us we are in a queuing system and
will be dealt with soon;
How many in the queue, one or fifty, they never tell you.
You try again later, to be told the same thing, until 5 pm,
Then an answerphone tells you the office is closed until 9 am tomorrow.
When trying to purchase something, you ask the price, you are told
the price,
On agreeing to buy the item, suddenly VAT comes into the equation,
The price was not the total price, another ploy to catch you out.
Junk Mail covers the carpet each day, most of it offering a service,
or inferior goods.
Bureaucracy is ruining our lives, destroying people's faith in a once
reasonable system.

There is so much *Red Tape* we may as well accept the fact.
Big Brother is not only watching us, but has truly taken over;
Data Bases know more about an individual, than that individual.
Nothing is sacred or private anymore, isn't it about time, we all united and said,
Enough is *Enough* thank you very much . . .

Amanda-Lea Manning

Paradise Lost

. . . death is more gratifying
than the slow dying of the heart
from sorrow and heartbreak

men have made this world
a hell for body and soul
an eternal self-inflicted pain
men are the doers of evil
the ultimate self-disintegrators
perpetrators of cruelty, injustice, misery
men are the beginning of the end
of this infinite universe
transformed into a heartless
insensitive mass of stones, meteorites
that have burnt the little
that was left of tears
and glutting the blood in veins
turning it to lifeless icicles

death is more gratifying
than the slow dying of the heart
from sorrow and heartbreak . . .

Raymond Fenech

My Pet Hates

I hated, when my husband died,
And we had to part,
Also folk, cruel to kids, and animals,
Because, they haven't, got a heart.

I also hate those, who are conceited,
And are always, looking in a glass,
For if they see, a mirror,
It's a thing, they cannot pass.

I hate people, who barge forward,
Instead of standing, in a queue,
Because they think, they are entitled,
To go, in front of you.

But the folk that I hate most,
Keep boasting, about their wealth,
But I'm not the least bit envious,
'Cos rather have, good health.

Jean Hendrie

Here

I hate this town, I hate this town
The small-minded people are getting me down
Leaving the countryside was a bit unjust
Here it is apathy, feelings of disgust
Days are the same, dirt and the grime
From the mouths of the people most of the time
No future I see as I live day to day
Deep down inside I may end up this way
I hate this town I hate this town
The small-minded people are getting me down
Some are drink crazy, some are just mad
Others are crying . . . it's all very sad
I hate this town I hate this town.

John Redmond

It Is Called Sport

Those posh, toffee nosed plums
Riding their horses
Chasing, shooting
Poor little fox cubs.
The hounds chase
To the sound of the horn.
How cruel!
These people derived from humanity,
This is not human,
This is not fair,
This is not sport.

Richard Ginn

Does He Take Sugar

I am no different
No different from you
So why can't you ask me
If it's one lump or two.

Why are you so afraid
So afraid of me
That you can't ask me
How I like my tea.

I don't know
Why you can't see
How you behave
Really hurts me.

By treating me different
You make me feel lame.
So show you understand
By treating me just the same.

I know you don't realise
That you act the way you do
But next time you make tea
It's one lump not two.

Ian Fowler

Room 101

A trip to London, Berkshire hotel
Changed days from the small motel
Booked into luxurious room 101
Shopping, shows and having fun
Cards for keys, how things change
No fumbling drunk, help rearrange

Night on the town, sumptuous food and wine
In trepidation, pretend I'm fine
Knowing my partner becomes Mr Hyde
Unlike the park, change like the tide
The demon booze in room 101
Private bar, the nightmare's begun

Makes no difference the luxury hotel
Booze is the same in a small motel
marble sinks with golden taps
Sadly for me my face took the raps
Some of the blows you could not see
Was the mental fatigue, that affected me

Eventually fleeing room 101
Hide in the corridors, space to run
Sitting in the lobby on a different floor
Jumping with fear to hear a door
Creep back to the room with the morning light
The sleeping drunk has lost the fight . . .

Jean Tennent Mitchell

WINTER WAKING

Huddled heat
wrapped in quilted slumber
snuggled deep
Shrieking alarm
pierces the veil
disturbing sleep
Energy sapping darkness
closing ranks
fights the waking
Reluctant limbs
emerge from the cocoon
warmth forsaking
Naked skin
clothed in apathy
chilling cold
Foggy mind, body weary
gripping fatigue
tightening hold
Shake the mood
seeking succour
crumpled clothing
Sleep-filled eyes
reflect rest denied
full of winter loathing
Comfort stolen
saddened features
stumble to work
Exposing elements
icy fingers hide
probing gathered murk.

Paul Birkitt

FACT OF LIFE

Legibus Parendum Est (The laws are to be obeyed)

I can't abide authority that tells me what to do
Or someone who vies my faith denying that it's true
My dreaded loathing fills me with thoughts of anarchy
My reasoning quells it with a fear of insecurity
Complicated co-existence, I crave for something new.

I can't abide authority that tells me what to say
Like someone who pushed me to say things just their way
My dreaded loathing fills my mind with nothing but contempt
My reasoning takes over for from these words I'm not exempt
Complicated co-existence, how I crave another day.

I can't abide authority that tells me how to act
Or someone who thinks he's God and shows a lack of tact
My dreaded loathing fills my soul with fiery hate
My reasoning gets into gear, suggesting I should wait
Complicated co-existence you are just another fact.

Timothy Alexander

Watcher

Giss a fag, gis a beer, ain't no fun around here.
Nowhere to go, nothin' to do, no one listens, not even you.
Can't change a thing, haven't a voice, got no choice.
Let's have a rave, let's misbehave, blow your mind babe.
Take a puff of this or a snort of that, think you've gone to heaven
and that's that -
Could take a course at college I guess, maybe, I could, catch up with
the rest.
Not sure I could cope with the test, but why not make myself a pest.
Given the knowledge, I can rebel, tell those politicians to go to hell.
I could make waves, I could have fun, I might even feel life has begun.
But I've got to take the first step.
All work and no play - is it for me -
What is my destiny?
Is it to be *Ecstasy,* could get the shakes and no even breaks.
Could my opinion turn into oblivion?
No, stuff your drugs, I'm not going yet.
I'm going to become teacher's pet.

IC

Just In Time

Drugs are lethal killers, it's a habit you must kick,
Remember your family suffers, when you are really sick,
Use all your strength to stop it now, don't make your families cry,
Give them a thought, they don't deserve the heartache when you die,
When you see others take them, just turn a blind eye,
Always remember one thing, you are too young to die,
So when you get to my age, think about this rhyme,
Then thank God that you stopped taking drugs *just in time.*

Barbara Fowler

An Alien View Of Life

'What a strange creature is man,' said the alien,
'Filling his mouth with unnecess'ry things.'
Helps me relax! Or *feel good*, their excuses
Wanting uniqueness, these hungry earthlings.

Lacking restraint in 'the good things', they clamour
For, eager to spider-web others to start;
'Ads' for tobacco, and alcohol drinking;
'Manly and - good for you - cool - and it's smart!'

As they grow older they learn that it's *not* true;
Heart disease, cancer, whilst liver and lung,
Hardened with such deleterious matter
Hasten their end whilst still biblic'lly young.

'That is not all,' said the wondering alien,
'See how like lemmings they clamour for drugs!
Reaching their brains to destroy them more quickly
- Change them to zombies - or inhuman thugs!

I must report to my world,' said the alien,
'Far too few savants within this doomed race.
No need to atomise these dang'rous people
- They kill off themselves at a quickening pace!'

M R Case

Colours High

Bleeding colours, Jacob's coat,
Round and round, and round they float,
Saffron yellow, crimson red,
Twisting, spinning, in my head,
Pearly, pulsing, purple dreams,
Soothing, moving, emerald greens,
Carmine tears, from weeping blues,
Swimming, mixing, multi-hues,
Twirling slow, my prism stone,
Popping pills, my mind has blown.

Gordon McDonald

Mum

Out on the street, she worked for her crack
Living for the moment, she never looked back.
Her child never mattered, she wound up in care.
An occasional mother, who was never really there
Feeding her habit, filling her arms with her 'food'
Like Jekyll and Hyde, she'd change her mood.
Happy when high, then low and depressed
Inside stayed her feelings, deep and suppressed.
Living in the fast lane, she just couldn't see
She was completely oblivious to reality.
Sinking lower and lower into her seedy state,
Coming around the corner was her tragic fate.
Her body was an engine, the drugs her fuel,
Her life was a mess, and her death was cruel.

M Bowler

Avian Traffic Casualty

Fledgling city-bound,
following used trails
bled dry and discarded.
Flying night blind,
thrust into the cocktail jazz
of a foul, sunk venue.
Burning lunar lamps bearing down,
wild eyes and staring veins
beat live-wire to the rhythmic tread.

Mute under the seeking glare of strobe,
frozen by dazzling arc lights.
Disorientated prey; shivering,
taut urban necks gape in anticipation.
She lies cold; twitching plume
entrails leave lines, incommunicable.
Anonymous carrion picked from the bone,
twisted graveyard dancing.

Simon Cox

CRACK KIDS

Crack kid spaced out in the park
Waiting for his drug-crazed friend
He's bringing more to leave their mark
On which both their lives depend

Crack kids then stagger around the town
Shouting abuse to everyone, life's a scream
Rebels smashing bottles playing the clown
Is this a nightmare, or an every day scene

Crack kids need to race stolen cars
Off their heads to the latest sound
Soon enough they crash leaving more scars
Their last trip leaves silence all around

Crack kids parents shoulder the blame
Our children's lives have ended this way
Broken hearts that will never mend again
Standing at the graveside on funeral day

M Morgan

Here Today, Gone Tomorrow

How sad it was
to see him fall
that tall dark teenager
who once had it all.

His brown eyes
which shone so bright
will no longer
see the light.

For he has taken
what I most fear
I tried to tell him
he did not hear

He surely threw
his life away
I watched it shorten
day by day.

Surely now,
we all must see
drugs are killers
and will always be.

Ciara O'Shaughnessy

MOTHER

You're hanging on to your life's thread
that's thinner than a spider's web
knowing that you must be home
in time for mother
methadone

checking time, your body clock
and nothing's going to make you stop
always waiting by the phone
- a call from mother
methadone

you never seem to count the cost
you didn't need the friends you've lost
now you want another loan
to pay your mother
methadone

in blanket darkness in the night
you're hot, you're cold, your breathing's tight
you're crying now, mind's all blown
you cry for mother
methadone

you're looking for that last escape
but even with the risks you take
love runs deep through blood and bone
you love your mother
methadone

P Adams

A Shoulder To Cry Upon

After a climb to four thousand feet,
By coach, and then more slowly on foot,
With the summer sun hot upon your back,
You finally look down into the mouth
Of a slumbering Vesuvius.

The cold hardened lava streams that still
Litter her sleep slopes are stark reminders
Of the awesome power that always lurks
Beneath you, and which, at long intervals,
Has brought destruction into so many lives.

Vesuvius in full eruption, with huge flames
And hot ash leaping enormous heights
Into the air, and with an unstoppable flow
Of her molten innards engulfing all lying
In its path, disgorges hell upon earth.

Like hers, my own emotional hell on earth
Is bottled up inside, a deepening anger
Just waiting to erupt, intent upon destroying
Only one life, as retribution for all the pain
And trauma heaped upon my disabled daughter.

In blacker moments, it does help to juxtapose
Past with present, and to imagine hurling him,
Her abuser, bodily into the fires of Vesuvius,
As my triumphant cry of 'Justice for Jackie'
Echoes out above roars from the inferno below.

Andrew Farmer

The Thatcherite Years

Workers in shipyards, steelworks and mines,
Housewives and children they all knew hard times.
But the hardest times were not hewn coal
It was the 'Thatcherite' years that put an end to it all.

Bludgeoned and beaten by her every decision
The people of the North no quarter were given
Orders sent out from her ivory tower,
How were such people given so much power?

Now the whole country sees what we've always known.
The blue flags hauled down the red flags being flown
For eighteen years she sat smug through it all,
Never giving a thought for those she put on the dole.

Even after her party ousted her out
Some of her cronies who revered her did shout
About her leadership qualities and political brain!
While the people of the North suffered the pain.

Patrick Humble

Tread Softly
(To Bill Barnes)

'Bye Bill.
I came today in prayer and thought
to say farewell. Dear friend, you know
I was with you in spirit? Can't
be nearer than that - even when
we meet again - at my coming
into those everlasting arms.
So glad to share earth's life and work -
to tread those tentative vital
early steps to eternity
with you, along the storm and peace.
'Bye Bill.

Robert D Shooter

Poems For A Friend

Through this restless world of trouble, we need a special friend
Someone we can depend on, and trust to the very end
A friend that stands by us, either through thick or thin
Someone that is faithful, and we can appreciate within

Even the secret heartaches, that lay heavy on our mind
Somebody that we can talk to, a friend so true and kind
As, a listening ear works wonders, whenever we feel low
A friend that we can turn to, whose loving ways will show,

If ever arguments occur, that can draw us back again
True friends will walk beside us, come sunshine, or even rain
But, why should good friends fall out, if God gives His direction
For He will lead the way, through His own protection

A friend is there to guide us, when we walk our daily path
Whenever sorrow arises, or when things just make us laugh
Whenever we go through troubles, and anxiety is there
A good friend we should rely on, and concerns they will share

We all need someone to show sympathy, whenever sorrows start
If we have a good friend, they will show a generous heart.
To the sense of understanding, and a friendly hand to touch
That speaks the words of knowledge, that means so very much

So, if we mix those good qualities, of kindness and affection
We need those things beside us, and powers of perception
If we have done wrong in the past, just leave them all behind
A good friend will never judge, humanity, we will find

If we thank God truly, and look up to Him through prayer
For bringing true friends close to us, and things show they really care
And thanking God most of all, for bringing that sweet union
To the truest friend that we possess, and happy communion.

Jean McGovern

BLACKIE

You were a stray in the driveway,
I heard you afar, meowing piteously under a car.
A little stray kitten, so sad and forlorn,
Looking at me - those eyes saying:
'Why have I been born, to be the cast-out after Christmas Day,
when the children have ceased from play?'

I crawled on my knees, to answer your pleas,
And safely took you away.

You stayed ever near as you still were in fear,
Lest you would be discarded again,
You purred and you played; charm and tricks you arrayed,
But your eyes were still clouded with pain.
My friends came to call; you were loved by them all;
With the old you would sit,
On their knees should they knit,
And with youngsters you'd play 'catch a ball'.

And then, as you grew, we wondered anew
As you happily sat on the mat -
A beautiful Persian! - Quite a new version
Of the dear little stray tattered cat.

You became my true friend, right up to the end.
When I was ill you lay on my bed.
You would not leave me, faithfully there to be -
Even if you weren't being fed.

We parted at last (the die had been cast!)
As I had to move from my home -
My friend took you in, so I waved goodbye with a grin,
As you would never again have to roam!

Beatrice Wilson

To A Good Friend - Janet

We met at school when we were young
And starting out in life:
We had our fights, we had our fun
And shared each passing strife.

We travelled then to work each day
Many miles upon the train;
We laboured at our daily grind
And shared the tedious strain.

The good times came - and bad times too;
My friend was always there;
How great it is to know that they
Just never ceased to care.

A helping hand they always gave,
A friendly listening ear,
For kindness is their special gift
For everyone to share.

Retired now we're free to enjoy
The slower pace of things;
But goodness me, my friend and I
Are running round in rings.

We're wanted here, we're needed there
Not a moment do we get
And through it all, in quiet times
Our friendship lingers yet.

Such friendship is a precious gift
Known to just a few.
For your friendship through the years
Jan- my thanks I give to you.

Mollie D Earl

Talking

Strangely,
I found a spider in my bed.
'Pardon me,' I said,
'But can I talk to you
About my holiday in Kent,
My mobile phone,
Or my moulded ornament?'

The spider wiped its legs
All over cotton sheets.
'Oh no,' it said in sunken voice with hairs stuck up,
And scurried into pleats.

I turned the TV on
And curled up in the bed
Shouting at the spider,
'Perhaps tomorrow I'll go and tell
My best friend instead.'

Doreen King

Remedy (For The Perfect Day)

I have envisaged my perfect day,
a day I believe perfect in every way,
here's an idea or two for the working man,
read below I've prescribed a plan -

Aboard my ship on a calm blue sea,
a cholesterol breakfast will do for me,
away from the papers - away from the telly,
I'll down the booze - put beer in my belly.

I cast out my float - I read my book,
I'm free from the rat-race - I know that much,
'Was that a bite? - maybe I dunno,
I'm in no hurry - I've no place to go.'

Gee this is paradise - can see mile upon mile,
I extinguish 'nother cigarette
think I'll go sleep for a while,
the hustle and bustle of life -
is an unnerving relentless assembly,
I'd best say 'bye bye' (au revoir) -
and thanks for the memory.

I yearn for nothing - I've no concern over money,
the normal day to day activities -
now seem a little funny,
I'm out of the rut - I seldom see the shops,
I'm living it up as much as I can -
boy this is the tops.

And as morn' turns to night - and I raise anchor,
it's back to base - back to my camper,
all in all I've had a jolly good time,
be same again tomorrow -
where there's no murder nor crime.

So put yourself in my shoes,
could you relate to this,
a life full of contentment -
of pure and unspoilt bliss,
if so - then there's one thing I must say,
this has become a remedy - for your perfect day . . .

Steven John Hatcher

The Golden Chain Of Friendship

Friendship is a golden chain
The links are friends so dear
Like a rare and precious jewel
It's treasured more each year,

And clasped together so firmly
With love that's deep and true
It's rich with happy memories
And fond recollections, too.

Time can't destroy its beauty
As long as memory lives
Years can't forget the pleasure
That the joy of friendship gives,

For friendship is a priceless gift
That can't be bought or sold
But to have an understanding friend
It's worth far more than gold,

And the golden chain of friendship
Is a strong and blessed tie
Binding hearts together
As the years go passing by.

Mary Chapman

Ellie

Don't be grateful
For the time I spend
With you,
For I need a friend too.
The love you give
You cannot measure.
Each friend is unique,
A very special treasure.
Constant as the sunrise
Through life's turbulent sea
Our friendship shall be,
That's a guarantee.
With love from the clown,
That's me.

Bernadette O'Reilly

FAIR HAIR

'Am I pretty Mum am I?
I'm clever too, I know it.'
Fair hair shining wide-eyed smile.
'Maybe, sometimes don't get vain.'

'I hate you Mum - let me go
Everyone else is allowed.'
Tousled fair hair, angry eyes.
'Not that disco at your age,
Wait another year or so.'

'He's gorgeous Mum. A real dish
And he fancies me I know.'
Neat fair hair and dreaming eyes.
'Bring him round when Dad's not in,
Then he won't see the nose stud!'

'Alright leave home if you must,
I can't stop you at sixteen.'
Candyfloss hair hard blue eyes.
'I hope you've taken advice,
And are safely on the Pill.'

Long fair hair and blue eyes closed.
Is this you? My lovely girl?
Lying dead on a cold slab.
Overdosed with Ecstasy.
All I feel is endless grief.
What a waste of life and youth.

Sheila Fernley

My Foolish Friend

How are you today my friend,
Where would you like to go
Or is your brain so muddled
You really do not know
You take your drugs so freely
You abuse your body so
So many people love you
But you really do not know
There are things out there for you to see
And places you could go
But you're locked inside your crazy mind
And you don't want to know
The drugs you take are killing you
Sometimes you're high then low
So many people love you
But you don't what to know
And when your drugs have killed you
And we have to say goodbye
How many friends will miss you
How many friends will cry
And we will sit and wonder
Why you self-destructed so
And still we'll always love you
But you will never know.

Gordon Outhwaite

ANIMALS IN CRISIS

I'm stuck in a room without any windows
there is no sun there is no light,
I'm stuck in a room without any caring I'm stuck here all alone,
Sitting in this room,
Panic is fear now hunger is anger and frustration is pain,
While the war is raging in the world outside we are all forgot!
Locked in a room full of fear and of anger trying to hold back the tears,
Locked in a room the size of a cupboard waiting for someone to hear,
What will they think when they open the door we are so shy and so thin
Stuck in a hell with nowhere to go stuck in a room with no way out,
Left here to die cos nobody loved us,
Our mum was taken at birth,
How long will we live how long till we die,
For perfumes and potions for you we must die,
Our lives are all pain with needles and
tubes stuck in our bodies for all to amuse,
We are all equal from a flea to a bat,
From a whale to a sea horse to the fish that swim back,
The bears in the snow the gulls in the air,
The rabbits the hamsters we are all there,
The dogs and cats they feel it too,
We all have emotion,
Including the pain of needles and tubes stuck in our brain,
We are all here think of us to what makes you superior
to an animal in a zoo,
Man is not right by making us cry one day you see,
Animals will take flight but until them you see,
Please think again of all the animals hurt in such pain,
As you wear cheap perfume and make-up the same,
And as for all men you can't say much aftershave hurts just as much,
So when you do shop until you drop,
Spray that perfume in your eyes then you can test before you buy!

Jodi Perkins

SPACE TRAVEL

What would it be like to travel out into space,
Leaving earth with little or no trace.
To find a planet where time stands still,
See glorious things and a lovely green hill.
Of meeting people of the lovely planet,
A lovely life, different habit.
Everything is friendly and full of grace,
if only I could travel out of space.
To watch the stars closer on the Milky Way
Wondering how long I could really stay.
Try to catch a falling star,
Seeing it travel fast and far,
Making friends with life on the planet,
Watch the earth come back into orbit
A good reason for being outerspace.

Margaret Upson

Sub-Millimetre Common User Bolometer Array

Scuba, scuba hidden star
Your veil was lifted from afar.
High on volcano's crusty rim
Your microwaves pulsated in.
Ten billion years travelled with ease,
Seduced by awesome expertise.
Primeval time within our sight
Without a twinkle, mighty light.

Shirley Johnson

NIGHT SKIES (TO SUSPECTING)

Do you watch the stars at night,
As they shine on me out of sight.
When there's no reason left to think,
Do you wish for something new to blink.
Am I hanging on the truths of lies,
While clarity away with you flies.
Are you out in space lost in vacuum,
With air exhaled and empty room.
Give the star that newly shines a name,
Unless it dwindles out, and I do the same.

Simon Long

FIREWORKS

(For Derek)

I see them now - the rockets,
Clusters of planets falling in the blue
Serenity of evening over trees
Clumped on a mound beside a placid lake,
And hear them yet
Exploding
Surprisingly in sequence to the gasps
Of those whose lives were ordered for an hour
By what it was had brought them out of doors,
Simple as children, sorrowful at last
The show was over, drifting home by dusk
Reluctantly as smoke and long ago -
That summer moment you, my brother, said
The stars were in our reach but fell away
Until the longest, brightest spark was dead.

Alasdair Aston

INFORMATION

We hope you have enjoyed reading this book - and that you will continue to enjoy it in the coming years.

If you like reading and writing poetry drop us a line, or give us a call, and we'll send you a free information pack.

Write to :-

Triumph House Information
1-2 Wainman Road
Woodston
Peterborough
PE2 7BU
(01733) 230749